14

The Bumblebee Queen

April Pulley Sayre

Illustrated by Patricia J. Wynne

ιⲁι Charlesbridge

The bumblebee queen
begins the spring
below ground
and all alone.

Bumblebees are native to North America, South America, Europe, and Asia. There are 250 bumblebee species.

She digs out. She flies.
Hungry, she seeks flowers.
She drinks nectar
with her long, hairy tongue.

She begins to search:
behind the barn,

beyond the lake.

She buzzes
around the bushes,

between the fields.

Bumblebees rarely sting. But they
will sting in defense and can sting
more than once.

She is looking for a place to build her colony.

A puddle?
No.

A bush?
No.

**An old mouse nest?
Yes!**

Bumblebees nest in the ground
or in sheltered, mossy, grassy
places such as old mouse nests or
abandoned birdhouses. Queens
have even nested in teapots!

Now she prepares.
She visits flowers and drinks nectar.
She gathers pollen.

She makes a waxy cup
called her honey pot.
In it she stores nectar
that she will eat on stormy days
when it is not
good weather for flying.

The bee's body produces wax that squeezes
out in little tiles from between the
segments of her abdomen. She pulls off the
tiles with her feet, and then chews them to
form her honey pot.

She forms some of the pollen into a lump.
She lays eggs in it and adds a wax covering.

After the eggs hatch, the queen chews
a small hole in the wax covering and
pushes in food to the larvae.

In five days, the eggs hatch.
They are lumpy, plump larvae.
No buzzing. No flying.
Just wiggling.

The larvae eat pollen.
The queen brings more.
The larvae grow, wriggling and chewing.

As the larvae grow bigger, the wax covering cracks. The queen repairs it and enlarges it.

Then, one spring day . . .
the larvae spin cocoons!

The larvae spin cocoons 10 to 14 days after hatching. The outer layers of silk harden and yellow, so the larvae no longer need the wax covering of the pollen clump for protection. The queen gets rid of the extra wax.

But the queen bee keeps working.
She collects nectar.
She gathers pollen.
She lays more eggs.

In between her other duties, the queen snuggles up to the new eggs. Heat from her body goes through a bare patch on her abdomen to warm the eggs.

In ten days, the cocoons ripen.
The queen chews them open.
Bees emerge, wings fanning!
Now the queen has helpers.

Worker bees are grey when they emerge, but their adult coloring starts to show in a few days.

The new workers gather nectar and pollen
and feed the larvae.

The first worker bees of the season are
the smallest. Later in the season, the
workers are bigger. This may be
partly because, as the colony grows,
more workers can gather more food for
the larvae.

Summer simmers.
The colony grows.
The queen lays more eggs.
Some form workers.
Some form drones.
Some will become new queens.

Workers are females that are smaller than the queen. Workers do the hive chores. Drones are stingless males whose only job is to mate, to help produce next year's bees.

Queen

Worker

Drone

A bumblebee colony can
contain from 30 to 400 bees.

In fall, nights chill and flowers shrivel.
New queens and drones emerge from the hive.

Scientists aren't sure what signals an egg to become a queen or a worker.

Drones from many colonies zoom across the fields,
dabbing drops of bee perfume.
New queens follow the perfume highways
to find drones and mate with them.

Workers, drones, and queens all eat nectar. Any extra nectar that is not eaten by the bees right away is kept in honey pots. As water evaporates from the nectar, it becomes honey.

The new queens drink nectar,
search for soft earth,
then dig down
to wait for spring.

While underground from fall to spring, the new queens go without food—sometimes as long as six months between meals.

But the workers, the drones,
and the old queen bee
stay aboveground.
They die.
They cannot survive the cold.

Old bee, queen of the bumblebees,
won't see next spring come.
But her daughters, the new queens,
will fly across the fields
and build colonies of their own.

In northern Canada, the entire bumblebee season is only a few weeks long. But in the southern United States, colonies may last for many months. Near the equator, bumblebee colonies may live year-round.

More Buzz about Bees

Almost 4,000 kinds of bees are native to the United States. Yet the bee that most people know, the honeybee, is not a native species; it was brought here by European settlers. Honeybees are used to make honey and to pollinate crops.

Native bees pollinate many plants that honeybees do not. Bumblebees can pollinate by a special process called "buzz pollination." When a bumblebee flies, its hair builds up a static charge. It enters the flower and grabs one of the flower's anthers (the long stalks that contain the pollen). The bumblebee shakes the anther and makes a loud buzzing noise. The pollen, shaken from inside the anther, is attracted by the electrostatic charge of the bee. So it jumps a short distance and sticks to the bee! Honeybees cannot pollinate eggplant and tomato flowers; bumblebees can. So whenever you eat a tomato . . . thank a bumblebee.

Good Bee-havior

- Plant a garden! You can enjoy it, and the bees can gather pollen and nectar from your plants. When possible, plant native plants—the kinds that have grown in your area for thousands of years. The native bees of your area depend on these kinds of plants. Avoid spraying pesticides in your garden.
- Get to know the different kinds of bees in your area. Most bees and wasps are gentle and rarely, if ever, sting. The key is to be calm and to look where you put your hands and feet. If you are observant, you will notice holes in the ground where bees or wasps come and go regularly. Avoid these places, which wasps or bees are likely to defend. It's safer to observe bees and wasps feeding on flowers.
- Some people are highly allergic to bee stings. If you are one of these people, you should be more cautious around bees of any kind.

For More Information

Books

Buchmann, Stephen L., and Gary Nabhan. *The Forgotten Pollinators.* Washington, DC: Island Press, 1997.

Glaser, Linda. *Brilliant Bees.* Brookfield, CT: Millbrook Press, 1993.

Griffin, Brian L. *Humblebee Bumblebee: The Life Story of the Friendly Bumblebees and Their Use by the Backyard Gardener.* Bellingham, WA: Knox Cellars Publishing, 1997.

Polacco, Patricia. *The Bee Tree.* New York: Philomel, 1993.

Sayre, April Pulley. *If You Should Hear a Honey Guide.* Boston: Houghton Mifflin, 1995.

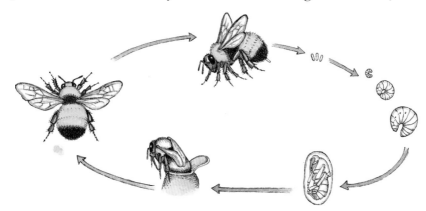

Websites

When searching for information, check under "bumblebees" or "native bees."

The Bumblebee Pages
http://www.bumblebee.org
This website contains extensive information on bumblebee biology.

The Xerces Society
http://www.xerces.org
This conservation organization focuses on insects. Its website has information on native bees.

The Arizona-Sonora Desert Museum
http://www.desertmuseum.org
This museum's website features information on native desert bees. (Search the site for "bees.")

To my fellow writers in The Hive: Carolyn Crimi, Jeanne Marie Grunwell, Phyllis Harris, Lindan Johnson, Laura Kemp, JoAnn Early Macken, Carolyn Marsden, David Masterton, Carmela Martino, Gretchen Will Mayo, Leslie Nydick, Mary Ann Rodman-Downing, Meribeth C. Shank, Marian Sneider, Gretchen Woelfle. Thank you for your support.—A. P. S.

For my mother, father, and sister with memories of the bee-filled fields of summer.—P. J. W.

Acknowledgments
The author would like to thank Dr. Jonathan Cnaani of the University of Toronto Department of Zoology and Dr. Gloria DeGrandi-Hoffman of the Carl Hayden Bee Research Center for reviewing various versions of this text.

Text copyright © 2005 by April Pulley Sayre
Illustrations copyright © 2005 by Patricia J. Wynne
All rights reserved, including the right of reproduction in whole or in part in any form. Charlesbridge and colophon are registered trademarks of Charlesbridge Publishing, Inc.

Published by Charlesbridge
85 Main Street
Watertown, MA 02472
(617) 926-0329
www.charlesbridge.com

Illustrations done in watercolor and ink on Arches paper
Display type set in Golden Type Bold and text type set in Adobe Caslon
Color separated, printed, and bound by Everbest Printing Company,
   Ltd., through Four Colour Imports Ltd., Louisville, Kentucky
Production supervision by Brian G. Walker
Designed by Susan Mallory Sherman

Library of Congress Cataloging-in-Publication Data
Sayre, April Pulley.
   The bumblebee queen / April Pulley Sayre ; illustrated by Patricia J. Wynne.
      p. cm.
Includes bibliographical references.
   ISBN 1-57091-362-5 (reinforced for library use)
1. Bumblebees—Juvenile literature. I. Wynne, Patricia, ill. II. Title.
QL568.A6S267 2005
595.79'9—dc22   2004003305

Printed in China
(hc) 10 9 8 7 6 5 4 3 2 1